Celtic Trail

Journey of Discovery

First edition published 2003

© CycleCity Guides 2003

Published by CycleCity Guides,
Wallbridge Mill,
The Retreat, Frome, BA11 5JU
Tel: 01373 543533.
www.cyclecityguides.co.uk

Printed by MWL Print Group Ltd,
Pontypool, South Wales.
Tel: 01495 750033

All pictures by Nick Cotton unless
otherwise stated.

All maps include data licensed from
Ordnance Survey® with the permission
of The Controller of Her Majesty's
Stationery Office.
© Crown Copyright 2003
Licence number: 43472U

ISBN 1 900623 16 1

Contents

Introduction

The Celtic Trail forms part of the National Cycle Network, the visionary scheme that aims to create a 10,000-mile network linking towns and cities throughout Britain by 2005. Opened in 2000, the Celtic Trail runs for 220 miles from the port of Fishguard on the coast of Pembrokeshire to Chepstow Castle, passing through a fantastic variety of scenery on its course from rural Pembrokeshire and Carmarthenshire through the old heartlands of industrial South Wales to journey's end in the medieval streets of Chepstow. Truly a journey of discovery.

The route has taken years of planning, negotiation, construction and signposting and is still an ongoing project. It links together quiet roads, roadside cycle lanes, converted railway paths, forestry tracks, canal towpaths and specially-built cyclepaths to create a thoroughly satisfying long distance route crossing the whole of Wales at its widest point.

It takes in St David's, Britain's smallest city, the spectacular Pembrokeshire Coast National Park, dramatic castles in Haverfordwest, Pembroke and Kidwelly, the magnificent Llanelli Millennium Coastal Park and the wide sweep of Swansea Bay before climbing to almost 2000ft on the beautiful and rugged High Level Route through the vast forestry holdings cloaking the hillsides between Neath and Pontypridd. Outstanding regeneration works have created a splendid and largely traffic-free route from Trelewis, north of Pontypridd, down through the wooded delights of Sirhowy Valley Country Park and along

Parc Slip Nature Reserve, near Tondu

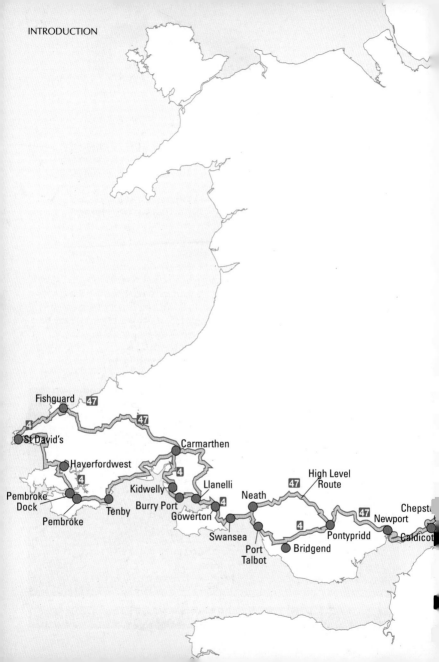

the towpath of the Monmouthshire & Brecon Canal into the heart of Newport. An amazing aerial trip on the Transporter Bridge takes you to the east side of the River Usk, leaving you with a few miles of easy and flat cycling to reach Chepstow and one of the finest castles in the whole of Britain.

Whether you choose to ride the whole route in one go, try a sample weekend on a part of the route or simply enjoy one of the many traffic-free sections that make an enjoyable day trip, this guide should help you to get more out of your journey, with details of refreshment stops, places of interest, train services and accommodation details.

How to use this guide

The book is laid out so that whether you are intending to do the whole of the Celtic Trail end to end, choosing a route for a 2-3 day trip or simply trying out one of the many traffic-free sections for a day ride, you can easily find the information you require.

ACCOMMODATION

The hotels, guest houses, Bed & Breakfasts, bunkhouses and other forms of accommodation listed in this guide have all been checked by the Wales Tourist Board. The list does not aim to be comprehensive, particularly in popular tourist centres, where there would just be too many establishments to list. A limited selection has been included for these resorts.

Local Tourist Information Centres can provide the most up-to-date information to help you find what you are looking for if you have any special requirements. The phone numbers (and where applicable, the email addresses) of the Tourist Information Centres along the route are listed under each section. Another useful source of information is the Wales Tourist Board website: www.visitwales.com

www.visitwales.com

7

STAGE		GRADE OF DIFFICULTY	MILES	PAGE
1	Fishguard* to Broad Haven	Strenuous	36	12
2	Broad Haven to Laugharne	Moderate/Strenuous	46	20
3	Laugharne to Kidwelly	Moderate	32	28
4	Kidwelly to Swansea (Mumbles)	Easy	29	36
5	Swansea (Mumbles) to Pontypridd (Quaker's Yard) via High Level Route	Strenuous	44	44
5A	Swansea to Pontypridd via the Southern Route	Moderate/Strenuous	40	52
6	Pontypridd (Quaker's Yard) - Chepstow	Easy	44	58
7	Carmarthen to Fishguard via the Preseli Hills	Strenuous	44	64
8	Carmarthen to Llanelli and Swansea	Moderate	42	68

There is only one train a day to Fishguard, arriving at approx 1330 hrs, so you may wish to go only as far as St David's (18 miles)

DOING THE WHOLE ROUTE FROM FISHGUARD TO CHEPSTOW

The route is described from west to east to make best use of the prevailing westerly winds. Apart from the very first stretch, from Fishguard to St David's, where you are heading almost due west and are likely to feel the wind strongly in your face, the winds should generally help you as you travel east towards Chepstow. The route has been broken down into six stages of 29-46 miles. You may wish to match these stages with each day's ride but this is only a suggestion: you may wish to do more or less than one stage per day. Stages 3 and 4 are short days (32 miles and 29 miles respectively) and you may link them together for a 61-mile day. There should be no problem finding accommodation in the first half of the ride, from Fishguard to Swansea. However, with the exception of Chepstow, the tourist infrastructure and the provision of accommodation in the second half is still in its embryonic stage so it is well worth booking ahead to ensure you have somewhere to stay.

At three points along the Celtic Trail you have a choice of taking a northern or southern route. To simplify the picture, imagine three circles in a row linked by a straight line: you could go along the top or along the bottom of the first circle. When you arrive at the next circle you have a similar choice. The route which is described most fully goes around the southern side of the first two circles and the northern side of the third: from Fishguard to St David's, Pembroke, Tenby and Carmarthen (end of the first circle) then south to Ferryside, Kidwelly and Llanelli (end of second circle). A short linear section links Llanelli through Swansea to the start of the Neath Canal (Briton Ferry) and the start of the third circle. Here it is suggested you take the (northern) High Level Route through the forestry to Pontypridd. From Pontypridd to Newport (via Trelewis, Hengoed, Sirhowy and Crosskeys) and on to Chepstow is once again a linear route.

The wooden walkway in Parc Slip Nature Reserve

Just to show you how a completely different route is possible: from Fishguard you could cross the dramatic Preseli Hills to Carmarthen, visit the National Botanic Garden at Middleton Hall, enjoy the 10-mile descent through Swiss Valley to Llanelli, follow the Llanelli - Swansea - Neath section (where there is no alternative) then staying on the southern alternative take in Margam Park, Parc Slip Nature Reserve and Tondu Iron Works before rejoining the first option described above from Pontypridd to Newport and Chepstow. As you can see, you have the option of two very different rides!

TWO OR THREE DAY SHORT BREAKS ALONG THE CELTIC TRAIL

There are various options for short breaks along the Celtic Trail: you may wish to do the western half of the trail in one trip and the eastern half at a later date; another possibility is to ride one of the various loops where two points on the Celtic Trail (for example Fishguard and Carmarthen) are connected by two different routes. Listed below are five suggestions for 2-3 day rides, two of which are linear, two of which are circular and one is lollipop-shaped, ie the first bit is used on both the outward and return trips.

1. FISHGUARD TO SWANSEA. 140 miles. Linear.

This is conveniently covered in its entirety by the *Celtic Trail - West* map. There is a daily train service from Swansea to Fishguard and fast and frequent services from all over the country to Swansea. If coming from a different part of the country it is cheaper to buy a return ticket to Fishguard than to buy a return to Swansea and a single on to Fishguard. See stages 1, 2, 3 and 4.

www.visitwales.com

9

The start of the Llanelli Millennium Coastal Park near to Pembrey

2. SWANSEA TO CHEPSTOW (VIA HIGH LEVEL ROUTE AND SIRHOWY COUNTRY PARK). 80 miles. Linear.

As above, conveniently covered by one map, this time the *Celtic Trail - East* map. There are fast and frequent train services from all over the country to Swansea. Chepstow is on the Newport to Gloucester line, so if you want to go to Bristol or London from Chepstow you will need to change at Severn Tunnel Junction. See stages 5 and 6.

3. CARMARTHEN TO FISHGUARD LOOP

(Carmarthen - Preseli Hills - Fishguard - St David's - Pembroke - Tenby-Carmarthen).

146 miles. Circular.

Covered by the *Celtic Trail - West* map. The longest of the three circular rides and the most spectacular, taking in the Preseli Hills and the Pembrokeshire coastline. Several trains per day from Swansea to Carmarthen. See stages 1, 2, 3 and 7.

www.visitwales.com

4. SWANSEA TO CARMARTHEN LOOP

(Swansea - Llanelli - National Botanic Gardens - Carmarthen - Kidwelly - Llanelli - Swansea).

86 miles.

Lollipop-shaped. Covered by the *Celtic Trail - West* map. The easiest of the three circular rides, with a long flat section from Ferryside and along the Millennium Coastal Park back to Swansea. There are fast and frequent train services from all over the country to Swansea. See stages 3, 4 and 8.

5. PONTYPRIDD TO NEATH LOOP

(Pontypridd - Tondu - Margam - Neath - High Level Route - Pontypridd).
66 miles. Circular.

Covered by the *Celtic Trail - East* map. There is a massive contrast between the wooded, sparsely inhabited northern section along the High Level Route and the rich industrial heritage of the southern route. Pontypridd is served by the Valley Lines service from Cardiff. See stages 5 and 5a.

DAY RIDES ON TRAFFIC-FREE SECTIONS OF THE CELTIC TRAIL

For more details of these rides see the relevant stage, ie the Brunel Way is in the Broad Haven to Laugharne Stage (page 20). For further information contact the Sustrans Information Service on 0845 113 0065 or visit www.sustrans.org.uk

COVERED BY THE *CELTIC TRAIL - WEST* MAP:

1. The Brunel Trail from Johnston to Neyland.
2. Kidwelly to the Wildfowl & Wetlands Centre
   (includes the Llanelli Millennium Coastal Park).
3. The Swiss Valley Trail from Llanelli to Tumble.
4. Swansea to Mumbles, along the sea front.
5. Swansea to Gowerton, via Clyne Valley Country Park.

COVERED BY THE *CELTIC TRAIL - EAST* MAP:

6. Neath Canal from Briton Ferry to Tonna.
7. High Level Route from Neath to Pontypridd (Llanwonno).
8. Pyle to Tondu through Parc Slip Nature Reserve.
9. Along Ogmore Vale from Brynmenyn to Nant-y-moel.
10. Taf Bargoed Community Park (Trelewis) to Hengoed.
11. Sirhowy Valley Country Park (Pontllanfraith to Cross Keys)
12. Cross Keys to the Fourteen Locks Visitor Centre
    (or into the centre of Newport) along the Monmouthshire
    & Brecon Canal towpath.

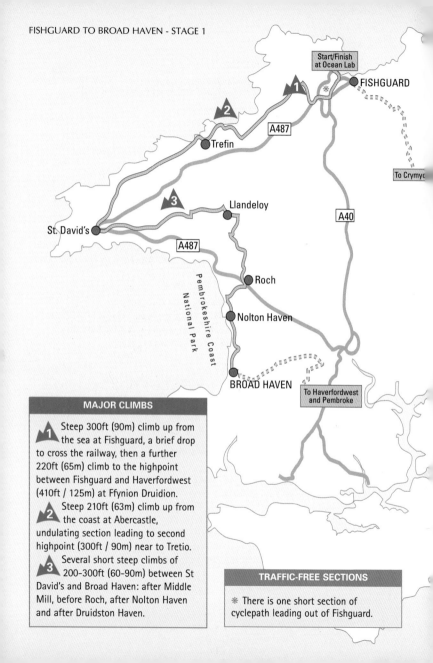

FISHGUARD TO BROAD HAVEN - STAGE 1

Start/Finish
at Ocean Lab

FISHGUARD

A487

Trefin

To Crymy

Llandeloy

A40

St. David's

A487

Roch

Pembrokeshire
Coast
National Park

Nolton Haven

BROAD HAVEN

To Haverfordwest
and Pembroke

MAJOR CLIMBS

1 Steep 300ft (90m) climb up from the sea at Fishguard, a brief drop to cross the railway, then a further 220ft (65m) climb to the highpoint between Fishguard and Haverfordwest (410ft / 125m) at Ffynion Druidion.

2 Steep 210ft (63m) climb up from the coast at Abercastle, undulating section leading to second highpoint (300ft / 90m) near to Tretio.

3 Several short steep climbs of 200-300ft (60-90m) between St David's and Broad Haven: after Middle Mill, before Roch, after Nolton Haven and after Druidston Haven.

TRAFFIC-FREE SECTIONS

✳ There is one short section of cyclepath leading out of Fishguard.

STAGE 1

Fishguard (Goodwick Harbour) to Broad Haven

36 MILES - STRENUOUS

The descent into Abercastle

The first section of the Celtic Trail takes you to the westernmost part of mainland Wales, running parallel to the stunning Pembrokeshire coastline all the way from Fishguard to St David's and on to Broad Haven. There are many highlights on this stretch but the dominating feature is the coast: what starts with the occasional glimpse of the Atlantic Ocean becomes a gently undulating ride to St David's with long unbroken vistas of the spectacular coastline.

Mention must be made of the wind - it blows most days and more often than not it blows from the west or southwest so the first 18 miles to St David's may be tough going. Beyond St David's you turn the corner and you now head in a generally easterly direction (with the prevailing winds on your back) all the way to Chepstow.

Fishguard lies at the end of the railway line and offers a ferry link across to Rosslare in the Republic of Ireland. An attractive mix of shops, cafes, pubs and other services cluster around the heart of the town. The town is in two parts: Goodwick lies right down by the sea and is where the railway station and ferry terminal are situated; Fishguard is up the hill a little way and is the commercial heart of the place.

The official start of the ride is from the Ocean Lab, near to the train station and ferry terminal in Goodwick. There is a fine network of quiet lanes lying between the main A487 and the coast and this is soon joined after a climb following the crossing of the railway. This is a land of solid stone farmhouses, stone walls, bright yellow gorse, fields of pasture and trees bent by the prevailing sea breezes. The sea lies below, glittering in the sunshine if you strike lucky with the weather! Up above, jets bound for America leave their trails high in the blue sky.

Several sharp descents take you down through wooded valleys close to the coast then there is a splendid downhill into the little cove at Abercastle. About 1/2 mile after Abercastle there is a turning off to the right to some of the best standing stones on the whole trip at Careg Sampson. The best opportunities for refreshments between Fishguard and St David's are to be found in the attractive little settlement at Trefin - there are a couple of tea shops and a pub. A fine tavern lies just off the route at Porthgain, a hamlet right on the coast to the north of Llanrhian. The way to St David's is now fairly flat and the route takes you in the back way, avoiding the A487 and approaching St David's Cathedral and the Bishop's Palace from the north.

 Public transport to Fishguard

There is a limited service from Swansea (one train a day arriving at about 1340 hrs).
National Rail Enquiries
Telephone: **08457 48 49 50**
Online: **www.nationalrail.co.uk** or **www.walesandborderstrains.co.uk**
Normally only two bikes are allowed on a train. You can make a reservation.

 Tourist Information

FISHGUARD
01348 873484
ST DAVID'S
01437 720392
HAVERFORDWEST
01437 763110
haverfordwestinformationcentre@pembrokeshire.gov.uk

Goodwick Harbour

Even if you are not spending the night in St David's it is worth setting by a morning or an afternoon to explore the place fully on foot. There are so many little streets and alleyways and lovely old buildings that it would be a real missed opportunity to whizz by without seeing it properly. If nothing else reward yourself with a good refreshment stop for having reached the most westerly city (!) in Wales.

The course of the Celtic Trail east from St David's has to divert inland as the main A487 runs along the coast. This is no hardship - the network of quiet lanes takes you though a rich and lush countryside that could have one of those 'places that time forgot' labels attached to it. There are two options between Llandeloy and Nolton Haven: if you are travelling east it is worth rejoining the coast at Penycwm / Newgale

(shortly after passing the five star-rated Penycwm Youth Hostel). This gives you a fantastic 300ft descent on the A487 through Newgale and along Newgale Sands. (If travelling west the steep climb up the A487 is best avoided by taking the inland route through Roch and Roch Bridge).

The inland and coastal routes link again just before Nolton Haven: there are wonderful views in all directions - Skomer Island lies to the south and Ramsey Island to the north. A series of short and steep climbs follows, one of which will take you past the extraordinary grass and glass structure near to the Druidstone Hotel. What views you must have from this unconventional conservatory! Make the most of the beach at Broad Haven, you won't be back by the seaside again until you reach Tenby.

Taking a dip near Nolton Haven

History and Background

This is a part of the world that has been welcoming visitors since the first pilgrims arrived in St David's in the Middle Ages. Known for centuries as 'Little England Beyond Wales', Pembrokeshire has a mixed Welsh and English heritage that has helped define it as a very different corner of the British Isles. The area's beautiful natural environment makes up the only coastal National Park in Britain. Generations of artists and craftspeople have found inspiration within Pembrokeshire and you can see this in the many galleries, potteries and craft centres throughout the region.

The area's rich Celtic legacy later mingled with a strong early Christian influence - saints such as St Non, St David and St Justinian were drawn to the area and of course St David's Cathedral is their most enduring legacy. In the Dark Ages the Vikings invaded and named the offshore islands and towns such as Tenby and Fishguard. They were followed in the 11th century by the Normans, who built Pembroke Castle, one of the most spectacular fortresses in Wales, and the birthplace of Henry Tudor, later King Henry VII.

An impressive line of castles and strongholds known as the Landsker Line divided Anglo-Norman Pembrokeshire in the south from Welsh Pembrokeshire in the north and even today Welsh-speaking areas are still mostly in the north. Pembrokeshire was also the site of the last invasion of Britain in 1797, near Strumble Head, commemorated in Fishguard by a skillfully-crafted tapestry.

www.visitwales.com

Wildlife

Wildlife thrives in the pristine environment around the Pembrokeshire coastline - Skomer and Skokholm islands have the world's largest colony of Manx shearwaters (150,000 pairs), Grassholm has the fourth largest gannet colony in the North Atlantic, and there is plenty of other birdlife such as puffins, cormorants, choughs, peregrine falcons, razorbills and oystercatchers. The wildflowers on the coast are in full bloom from April to June, coinciding in late spring with the annual invasion all along the coast as thousands of seabirds return to nest. Ramsey Island is famed for its grey seals, and dolphins and porpoise are also common in the area, whilst more exotic marine visitors include basking sharks, whales and sunfish.

Places of interest

FISHGUARD

Fishguard's Welsh name is Abergwaun, meaning 'mouth of the River Gwaun'. The prettiest part of Fishguard - known as the Lower Town or Lower Fishguard - is clustered around the old quayside where the Gwaun flows into the sea. Its row of harbourside cottages is wonderfully photogenic - a quality exploited by the makers of the film of Dylan Thomas's *Under Milk Wood*, starring Elizabeth Taylor and Richard Burton, when Lower Fishguard became the imaginary seatown of Llareggub.

GOODWICK

The modern port, with ferry services to Rosslare in the Irish Republic, is a purpose-built harbour, created in the early 20th century, just across the bay from Lower Fishguard.

LAST INVASION TAPESTRY

An ill-equipped French force, led by an

Irish-American general, landed at nearby Carregwastad Point on 22nd February 1797. The 'invasion' was a short-lived affair, the French surrendered without engaging in conflict. St Mary's Church has a tombstone to Jemima Nicholas, a formidable local character who captured 12 Frenchmen single handed, armed only with a pitchfork!

TREGWYNT WOOLLEN MILL
A whitewashed mill in a lovely spot dating from the 18th century. It is a working mill producing traditional Welsh weaves.

LLANGLOFFAN FARMHOUSE CHEESE CENTRE
Demonstrations of the three stages of cheesemaking, made from the milk of the farm's own herd of cows.

ABERCASTLE
Lime kilns and old warehouses point back to the days when the rocky inlet was a coastal trading port dating back to Tudor times. From here it is a short walk westwards to Careg Sampson, a Stone Age burial chamber.

ST DAVID'S
With its 12th-century cathedral, St David's can proudly claim to be Britain's smallest city! The cathedral was originally founded in the 6th century by St David. The present

Bike Shops

Premier Sports (limited repairs)
High Street, Fishguard
01348 873880

St Davids Cycle Hire (limited repairs)
01437 721911

Haven Sports
Marine Road, Broad Haven
01437 781354

cathedral was begun in the 12th century. In the Middle Ages two pilgrimages to St David's were said to be the equivalent of one to Rome, with three accounting for one visit to Jerusalem. Amongst the great glories of the cathedral are an ornately carved roof of Irish oak and the original late-Norman nave. The ruined Bishop's Palace in the field opposite the cathedral now has the look of a poor relation, though in its prime it would have been a very grand and desirable residence. Built in the 13th and 14th centuries, its opulent style reflected the worldly wealth of the medieval church.

RAMSEY ISLAND
If you are staying overnight in St David's during the summer you may wish to make a boat trip from Porthstinian to Ramsey Island, a holy island created in legend by the 6th-century Breton saint, Justinian, who axed it from the mainland to ensure solitude.

Refreshments

FISHGUARD
Lots of choice

TREGWYNT
Woollen Mill

TREFIN
Glan y Mor Gallery &
Tearoom, Ship Inn, Melin
Trefin Craft Shop &
Tearoom

LLANRHIAN
Artramont Arms
(also does cream teas)

PORTHGAIN
(just off the route)
The Sloop Inn, fine pub on
the coast. Cafe

RHOSYGILWERN
Dairy / Perennial Nursery
and Tearoom (4 miles north
of St David's)

ST DAVID'S
Lots of choice

MIDDLE MILL
WOOLLEN MILL
Open all year Mon - Fri.
From Easter to the end of
Sept open on Sat 9.30-
5.30pm and Sun 2-5.30pm

NEWGALE
Pebbles Cafe

ROCH
Victoria Inn,
Roch Gate Motel

NOLTON HAVEN
Mariners Inn

BROAD HAVEN
Galleon Inn, The Royal,
Seaview Cafe

Accommodation

FISHGUARD
**Hamilton Backpackers
Lodge**
Hamilton Street
01348 874797

Cri'r Wylan
01348 873398

Abergwaun Hotel
Market Square
01348 872077

Cartref Hotel
High Street
01348 872430

Avon House
High Street
01348 874476

Seaview Hotel
Sea Front
01348 874282

GOODWICK
Pwll Deri Youth Hostel
01348 891385

**Ferryboat Inn &
Restaurant**
St Davids Road
01348 874747

Glanmoy Lodge GH
Tref-Wrgi Road
01348 874333

Fishguard Bay Hotel
Quay Road
01348 873571

Ivybridge
Drim Mill
01348 875366

TREFIN
Trefin YHA
01348 831414

Annies B&B
North End
01348 837116

Bryngarw GH
Abercastle Road
01348 831211

ST DAVID'S
St David's YHA
Whitesands Bay
01437 720345

Alandale GH
Nun Street
01437 720404

The Waterings
Anchor Drive
01347 720876

Cwmwdig Water GH
Berea
01348 831434

PENYCWM
Youth Hostel
Penycwm
01437 721940

BROAD HAVEN
Anchor GH
The Seafront
01437 781476

Lion Rock GH
Haroldston Hill
01437 781645

Atlantic View B&B
Settlands Hill
01437 781589

Albany B&B
Millmoor Way
01437 781051

MAJOR CLIMBS

1 There is a 375ft (115m) climb up from Broad Haven.

2 The climb from Haverfordwest to the highpoint just south of Dreenhill is separated into two parts with a dip in the middle: a 195ft (60m) climb to Dreenhill then, after crossing Merlin's Brook, a 150ft (45m) climb to the highpoint.

3 The next climb, of 315ft (96m) comes between Pembroke and St Florence up onto the Ridgeway.

4 A 325ft (99m) climb takes you from Tenby up and over to Saundersfoot. Part of this is on a track where you may prefer to walk.

5 The steepest and highest hills of the day come after Amroth. The first rises 465ft (141m) up from the sea at Amroth Castle, the second, of 370ft (113m) between Marros and the crossing of the B4314.

TRAFFIC-FREE SECTIONS

* The railway path from Johnston to Neyland (Brunel Cycle Route).

** One short section at the edge of Tenby, two short stretches between Saundersfoot and Amroth.

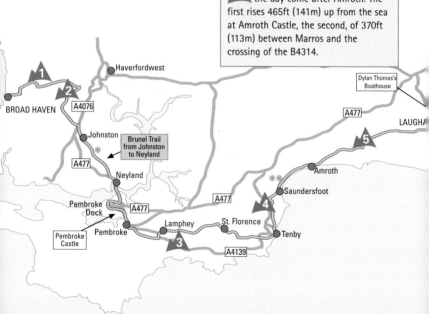

STAGE 2

Broad Haven to Laugharne

46 MILES - MODERATE/STRENUOUS

The traffic-free promenade east of Saundersfoot

This stage takes you past the mighty castle in Pembroke, touches the coast in Tenby and Saundersfoot and, after the toughest hills on the whole of the section between Fishguard and Swansea, drops down into the delightful coastal village of Laugharne, made famous by its association with the poet, Dylan Thomas.

The Celtic Trail turns inland from Broad Haven: the massive natural harbour of Milford Haven, which has become a major port for tankers bringing crude oil to the refineries, acts as a barrier to land travel from the west to the east: the bridge at Pembroke Dock (used in the ride) is the only crossing between the A40 near Haverfordwest and the Atlantic Ocean.

The trail climbs eastwards from the coast towards Haverfordwest, with its castle and museum. A spur from the main Celtic Trail leads into the centre of town. The first long traffic-free section of the Celtic Trail comes soon after Haverfordwest. At Under the Hills Lane a restored masonry bridge over the Merlin's Brook takes you to a brand new route through fields, following a Norman mill leat and along the valley to Cinnamon Grove. A short temporary on road section leads to a bridle path through the beautiful Bolton Hill woods (path upgraded and surface dressed with gravel) and on to Johnston where a new section alongside the railway leads to the centre of the village.

The second, longer part starts somewhat improbably from the back of a small housing estate in Johnston. The trail runs gently downhill along the course of a disused railway south to Neyland, passing through Westfield Pill Nature Reserve. This traffic-free path is a real highlight of the section, passing through attractive woodland with views downhill into the valley and ahead to the marina. It is worth visiting the marina to see the array of colourful boats and take refreshments at the Yacht Haven Bar.

 Public transport to Haverfordwest

Wales & Borders Trains from Swansea to Haverfordwest.
National Rail Enquiries
Telephone: **08457 48 49 50**
Online: **www.nationalrail.co.uk** or **www.walesandborderstrains.co.uk**
Normally only two bikes are allowed on a train. You can make a reservation.

 Tourist Information

Haverfordwest
01437 763110
haverfordwestinformationcentre@pembrokeshire.gov.uk
Pembroke
01646 622388 (seasonal)
Tenby
01834 842402
Saundersfoot
01834 813672 (seasonal)
Carmarthen
01267231557
carmarthentic@carmarthenshire.gov.uk

All good things must end and the high bridge over the creek is the signal for you to leave the cyclepath and climb steeply up the track which leads to the road and the two bridges that take you into Pembroke Dock and Pembroke. Your eventual goal through this urban section is the mighty castle in Pembroke. There are, however, many streets and turnings to negotiate before you get here so have your wits about you right from the moment you cross the main bridge: keep a sharp lookout for signs and have the map handy!

Pembroke Castle was one of a line of castles in Pembrokeshire that protected this small English enclave known as 'Little England beyond Wales'. The well-designed cyclepath contours around the edge of the moat allowing you fine views of the castle from almost all sides.

The quiet lane network is rejoined to the east of Pembroke and followed through Lamphey up on to the Ridgeway where coastal views open up once again. St Florence is an attractive village down off the Ridgeway and a possible overnight stop for those who wish to avoid the hustle and bustle of Tenby and Saundersfoot.

As with Pembroke, the route into and through Tenby requires extra attention and sharp vision to spot the signs! You arrive at the edge of town having passed the golf course and come to a T-junction by an establishment called 'The Night Owl' which is billed as 'South Wales Premier Night Club'! One wonders what they would make of that in Swansea and Cardiff! Tenby is a busy seaside resort with all the services and entertainments one might expect to find. If for reasons of time or choice you do not wish to visit Tenby there is an obvious shortcut from St Florence to Saundersfoot on quiet lanes.

Tenby and Saundersfoot are two of the most popular seaside destinations in Pembrokeshire. Protected from the prevailing westerly winds and boasting a whole string of fine sandy beaches overlooking Carmarthen Bay, they are far less exposed than the beaches near to St David's which face the Atlantic. Tenby is a walled town with many fine buildings and a great place to explore on foot. It is worth locking up your bike and going for a stroll around the fascinating streets. If, however, the weather is hot enough to tempt you into the sea for a dip, on your bike you are in a position to escape the crowds and find more secluded beaches.

Two short offroad sections after Saundersfoot, the first involving tunnels where you are asked to dismount and push your bikes, keep you close to sea level and avoid the need to climb two hills. This is the only place on the ride where the Celtic Trail shares an offroad, traffic-free section with the Pembrokeshire Coastal Path. You should be grateful for being spared these hills as those that you face between Amroth and Laugharne are the longest on the whole Fishguard - Pembroke - Swansea section! A fast descent after the church at Marros down to the Green Bridge Inn separates the two climbs.

You are wonderfully rewarded for all your efforts: the 4-mile descent into Laugharne is the stuff of which dreams are made and Laugharne itself is a very attractive stopping point either for refreshments or for an overnight stay. Made famous by

Massive chimneys in the village of St Florence

Dylan Thomas, Wales' most celebrated poet, it is a fine little fishing village with a castle, extensive views over the Taf estuary and a wide selection of cafes, pubs and wine bars.

Places of interest:

HAVERFORDWEST
High above the town, Haverfordwest's 12th-century castle offers panoramic views of the western arm of the Cleddau River and the surrounding countryside. The stonework that has survived is exceptionally strong, defeating even the attempts made by Cromwell's men to demolish the castle during the Civil War. The castle stands next to a squat stone building that once served as a gaol which now houses the the Castle Museum and

www.visitwales.com

23

Art Gallery. Haverfordwest was a thriving port from late medieval times: the western Cleddau was once navigable all the way to the town, giving the town access to the Milford Haven waterway. Echoes of the town's sea-trading days remain along the Old Quay.

NEYLAND

An old seafaring town and railway port of neat terraces on a hillside above the Milford Haven waterway. The waterfront is called Brunel Way in memory of the great Victorian engineer, Isambard Kingdom Brunel, whose Great Western Railway reached Neyland in 1856. From here passengers sailed on to southern Ireland. The Cleddau Bridge, a crucial road link

 Bike Shops

Haven Sports
Marine Road, Broad Haven
01437 781354

Mikes Bikes
17 Prendergast, Haverfordwest
01437 760068

Halfords Superstore
Bridgemeadow Lane, Haverfordwest
01437 767313

Enterprise Cycles
Unit 40 Honeyborough Ind Est, Neyland
01646 601014

Bierspool Cycles
London Road, Pembroke Dock
01646 681039

Tenby Cycles
The Norton, Tenby
01834 845573

Cross Inn Stores
The Grange, Saundersfoot
01834 813266

between the south and north banks of the waterway, was opened in 1975, replacing the ferry that used to run between Neyland and Hobb's Point.

PEMBROKE CASTLE

Pembroke Castle was an early power base for the Norman invaders. Its present appearance is due to William Marshall, an influential English knight who rebuilt the fortress in the late 12th and early 13th centuries. His magnificent castle, on a wooded outcrop above the streets and river, remains unaltered to this day. Its size only becomes fully apparent when you walk through its Great Gatehouse. The castle walls enclose a large grassy inner ward dominated by the Great Keep, a huge round tower nearly 80ft high. The castle is reputed to be the birthplace in 1457 of Henry VII, the Welshman who became the first of the Tudors.

ST FLORENCE

This charming little village gained importance in the 12th century when Norman kings encouraged people from Flanders to settle here. A small cottage near the church has two enormous Flemish-style chimneys. In amongst the narrow lanes several buildings have stone-framed doorways with pointed arches.

TENBY

Tenby's beautiful harbour is overlooked by Georgian and Regency buildings. Its history dates back still further: the church was built in the 13th century and there are ruins of a castle and a medieval jumble of narrow thoroughfares encircled by well-preserved ancient town walls. There are many fine old buildings in the town, particularly the Tudor Merchant's House, a tall, three-storeyed late 15th-century building which is probably the oldest

Westfield Pill Nature Reserve fom the Brunel Trail

surviving dwelling in Tenby. Tenby was also an early resort, attracting visitors from the latter part of the 18th century when sea-bathing first became fashionable. The two main beaches of South Sands and North Sands may well tempt you off your bikes and in for a dip if the weather is hot and sunny. It is your first chance since leaving Broad Haven.

SAUNDERSFOOT

The resort's capacious harbour is one of the most popular sailing and watersports centres in South Wales. Wiseman's Bridge, a little way along the coast, has a small steep beach on which the D-Day landings were rehearsed, watched by Winston Churchill. Landwards, Saundersfoot is almost encircled by wooded hills.

AMROTH

This village is the starting point of the Pembrokeshire Coastal Path which runs for 168 miles around to Cemmaes Head near to Cardigan. The petrified stumps of an old forest, drowned 1000 years ago, can be seen on the beach at Amroth at low tide. The woods above Amroth contain the Colby Woodland Garden, with a walled garden, kitchen garden, Gothic gazebo and seasonal displays of daffodils, rhododendrons and azaleas.

LAUGHARNE

No one has captured the atmosphere of this sleepy sea-town on the Taf estuary better than its most famous resident, writer and poet, Dylan Thomas. Laugharne was the 'timeless, mild, beguiling island of a town', the place where Dylan 'got off the bus and forgot to get on again'. He lived at The Boathouse, his 'house on stilts' by the swirling silent sea and sands of the estuary's 'heron-priested shore'.

The spirit of Laugharne, which mingled in

Pembroke Castle

his mind with memories of the time he spent at New Quay on Cardigan Bay, inspired the writing of his most famous work, *Under Milk Wood*. This 'play for voices' is a mesmerising day in the life of a mythical Welsh coastal community called Llareggub, populated by such characters as Captain Cat, Mrs Ogmore-Pritchard and Willy Nilly, the postman.

Some of Dylan's happiest, most productive times were spent at Laugharne. He died in New York in 1953 and is buried in Laugharne's churchyard. Today the Boathouse is a Heritage Centre dedicated to his life and work. The Castle, within walking distance of The Boathouse, overlooks the Taf estuary. It is of medieval origin with Tudor additions.

Refreshments

HAVERFORDWEST
Lots of choice

DREENHILL
Masons Arms PH

JOHNSTON
Railway PH

NEYLAND
Neyland Yacht Haven Bar
(1/2 mile diversion from
the route)

**PEMBROKE DOCK AND
PEMBROKE**
Lots of choice

LAMPHEY
Lamphey Hall Hotel, Court
Hotel, Dial Inn

ST FLORENCE
Parsonage Farm Inn, Sun
Inn, New Inn, stores

TENBY
Lots of choice

SAUNDERSFOOT
Lots of choice

AMROTH
Amroth Arms PH, Pirate
Cafe, New Inn (at the east
end of village)

LAUGHARNE
Lots of choice

Accommodation

PEMBROKE DOCK
**Pembrokeshire
Watersports**
Fishguard Harbour Centre
01646 622013

LAMPHEY
High Noon GH
01646 683736

ST FLORENCE
**Greenhills Country
Hotel**
01834 871291

Parsonage Farm Inn
01834 871436

Flemish Court GH
01834 871413

TENBY
Paragon House B&B
The Paragon
01834 843022

The Broadmead Hotel
Heywood Lane
01834 842641 / 843361

Gumfreston Hotel
Culver Park
01834 842871

Sunnybank GH
Harding Street
01834 844034

Southcliff Hotel
Victoria Street
01834 842410

Clarence Hotel
Esplanade
01834 844371

Blue Dolphin Hotel
St Mary Street
01834 842590

SAUNDERSFOOT
Cliff House
Wogan Terrace
01834 813931

Harbourlight GH
High Street
01834 813496

The Lanterns
Milford Terrace
01834 814999

Claremont Hotel
St Brides Hill
01834 813231

WISEMAN'S BRIDGE
Pinewood B&B
Cliff Road
01834 811082

LAUGHARNE
Laugharne Castle GH
Market Lane
01994 427616

Swan Cottage B&B
Gosport Street
01994 427409

MAJOR CLIMBS

1 There is a climb of 270ft (82m) between Laugharne and St Clears.

2 Following St Clears there is a short undulating section then a steep climb (460ft /140m) up from the bridge over the Afon Cywyn at Pont-ddu.

3 The only major climb, to the south of Carmarthen, comes in two parts, separated by a sharp dip near Croesyceiliog: the first part is 165ft (50m) and the second 425ft (130m).

TRAFFIC-FREE SECTIONS

* One short stretch on the approach into Kidwelly.

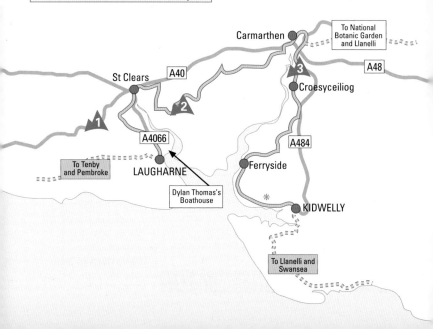

STAGE 3

Laugharne to Kidwelly

32 MILES - MODERATE

St Ishmaelis Church, south of Ferryside

The course of this section of the Celtic Trail is largely dictated by the crossing of two of the major rivers of southwest Wales: the Taf and the Tywi. The bridges in St Clears and Carmarthen are the earliest points at which it is possible to cross the rivers. Between the two crossings is a delightful area of lush fields, attractive hamlets and remote farmhouses. After reaching Kidwelly there are no hills worth mentioning until well to the east of Swansea.

After leaving Laugharne the next main settlement is St Clears and there are plans in the future to avoid spending any time near the fast and busy A40 by creating a link from the south end of the village to Ty'r Gate (see the proposed route on the Celtic Trail map). Once beyond St Clears, the lane network to the south of the A40 passes through an area which has the feel of a cut-off peninsula, if not an island: all the main through traffic bypasses the

Looking across to Llansteffan Castle from Ferryside

 Public transport to Laugharne

There is no train station at Laugharne. The nearest is at Whitland (reached from Swansea), then follow the B4328 and B4314 south and southeast through Red Roses to join the Celtic Trail about 5 miles west of Laugharne.

National Rail Enquiries
Telephone: **08457 48 49 50**
Online: **www.nationalrail.co.uk** or **www.walesandborderstrains.co.uk**

Normally only two bikes are allowed on a train. You can make a reservation.
Other useful train stations:
Carmarthen
Ferryside
Kidwelly

 Tourist Information

CARMARTHEN
01267231557
carmarthentic@carmarthenshire.gov.uk

 Bike Shops

Hobbs Cycles
Johnstown, Carmarthen
01267 236785

Ar De Feic
Heol Y Brenin, Carmarthen
01267 221182

Halfords Superstore
Parc Pensarn, Carmarthen
01267 237087

www.visitwales.com

30

triangle of land that is bounded by the River Taf to the west, the River Tywi to the east and the A40 to the north and as a result there is an unspoilt charm about the rolling country lanes through this lovely wooded area.

Depending on your itinerary, Carmarthen may represent somewhere just short of the halfway stage on your journey from Fishguard to Chepstow or the end of the road as you finish the loop that has taken you from Carmarthen to Fishguard via the Preseli Hills, returning along the Pembrokeshire Coast. For those of you who have opted to do the linear route from Fishguard to Chepstow you can start planning now to return to this beautiful part of the world and see all those things you missed first time round on the other alternative!

County Hall, Carmarthen

Overlooking the Tywi Estuary south of Ferryside

The church in Ferryside

From Carmarthen there are two routes to Llanelli. The northern route, described on page 68, visits the National Botanic Garden and descends into Llanelli via the traffic-free railway path down Swiss Valley. The southern route described here closely follows the Tywi estuary then the coast. It is during this section that the character of the Celtic Trail changes: whereas up till this point it has been predominantly on quiet country lanes it now starts using a higher proportion of traffic-free paths built through areas newly landscaped and regenerated after the demise of the region's heavy industries. Having said all that, after leaving Carmarthen, some of the country lanes that are followed towards Ferryside are so quiet there is a veritable garden growing up in the middle of the road! You descend to Ferryside with a chance of refreshment and great views across the Tywi estuary to Llansteffan Castle.

Another extraordinary building - St Ishmaels Church - is passed shortly after leaving Ferryside. An attractively designed traffic-free path across meadows with views across to Kidwelly Castle takes you right into the heart of the town and over the bridge spanning the Gwendraeth Fach.

Kidwelly Castle

Places of interest

CARMARTHEN

Situated on a bluff above the River Tywi, which rises in the Cambrian Mountains in the heart of Mid Wales, Carmarthen is dominated by the ruins of its Norman castle. It was the site of Moridunum, the Romans' most westerly fortress in Britain and there is still a large amphitheatre to the east of the town. In modern times the town has developed as a county town, marketplace and commercial centre for the region where the predominant industry is agriculture.

Oriel Myrddin Art Gallery

A contemporary craft and regional art gallery with changing exhibitions.

Heritage Centre

This exciting development on the banks of the River Tywi traces Carmarthen's history from AD75 to the present day.

Old town walls in Kidwelly

The famous Ferry Cabin in Ferryside

FERRYSIDE

The village stands close to the junction of the Tywi, Taf and Gwendraeth rivers which form a fork-shaped waterway flowing into Carmarthen Bay, bordered by sands, saltmarshes and green farmlands. There are magnificent views across the estuary. The rocky foreshore below the hill is the site of the vanished village of Hawton, destroyed in a huge storm about 300 years ago.

KIDWELLY

The town has one of the best preserved castles in Wales, standing on a steep ridge above the river. The castle, with its massive towers, dates back to the 12th century. Below its walls the 14th-century bridge spans the little Gwendraeth Fach river. Fragments of the fortified medieval town survive amongst Kidwelly's streets. The Kidwelly Industrial Museum is the only place in Wales where you can see how tinplate was made by hand.

Refreshments

LAUGHARNE
Lots of choice

ST CLEARS
Lots of choice

CARMARTHEN
Lots of choice

FERRYSIDE
Lion Hotel, Ship PH, Ferry Cabin, stores

KIDWELLY
Lots of choice

Accommodation

LLANGYNOG

Plas Farm
01267 211492

Wern Inn
01267 241678

CARMARTHEN

The Drovers Arms Hotel
Lammas Street
01267 237646

Y Dderwen Fach GH
Priory Street
01267 234193

Meiros Hall B&B
Waterloo Terrace
01267 222708

FERRYSIDE

Greenfields Cottage B&B
01267 267815

KIDWELLY

Penlan Isaf Farm GH
01554 890084

Glangwendraeth Farm GH
Priory Street
01554 890309

MAJOR CLIMBS

The route is flat with the exception of a small 195ft (60m) climb in Gowerton.

TRAFFIC-FREE SECTIONS

Most of the Celtic Trail between Kidwelly and Swansea is traffic-free.

✳ The first 14-mile traffic-free section runs from the A484 just south of Kidwelly, through Pembrey Forest, Burry Port and Llanelli to the Wildfowl & Wetlands Centre. There is a short stretch (about 3/4 mile) on quiet lanes through Burry Port.

✳✳ There is an 8-mile traffic-free section from Gowerton through Clyne Valley Country Park to Swansea Bay and along the Promenade into the heart of Swansea.

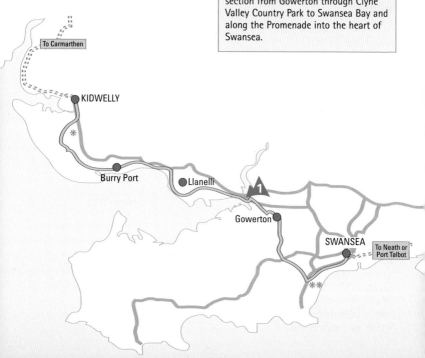

STAGE 4

Kidwelly to Swansea

29 MILES - EASY (the easiest stage on the whole of the Celtic Trail)

Soon after Kidwelly, at the end of the cycle path alongside the A484, you drive off improbably under a low bridge beneath the railway line to emerge into a different world of rough pastures and the extensive woodland of Pembrey Forest. As a result of problems with the water table, which leads to occasional flooding in the forest, you may be directed on to an alternative route which runs closer to the line of the A484. Whichever route you take, you soon reach one of the highlights of the whole Celtic Trail - the Llanelli Millennium Coastal Park, stretching from Pembrey Country Park to Loughor.

Massive regeneration and earth-moving has transformed the area in the past few years into one of the most popular cycling trails in Wales with thousands of people out on fine weekends rediscovering the joy of cycling along a safe and flat traffic-free trail with the wind in their hair and fine views across to the Gower Peninsula. The sand dune section at the start of the Coastal Park is a Site of Special Scientific Interest (SSSI). Soon after this you cross the two mighty land bridges that have been built to cross over the railway line. There are several pieces of outstanding sculpture along this section. At Sandy

Llanelli Millennium Coastal Park

National Rail Enquiries
Telephone: **08457 48 49 50**
Online: **www.nationalrail.co.uk** or
www.walesandborderstrains.co.uk
Normally only two bikes are allowed on a train. You can make a reservation. Other useful train stations: Ferryside, Llanelli, Burry Port, Swansea (which is served by several train companies).

 Tourist Information

LLANELLI
01554 772020
SWANSEA
01792 468321
tourism@swansea.gov.uk

Water Park in Llanelli you have a choice of completing a 52-mile circuit that links back to Carmarthen (via a traffic-free trail up through Swiss Valley and past the Cwm Lliedi Reservoirs, described on page 68) or of continuing east towards Swansea.

The route to the east goes past the superbly set Wildfowl & Wetlands Centre which has started attracting back many species of bird not seen in these parts for decades. A safe crossing of the A484 via a new pedestrian bridge leaves you with a few miles on road, into Loughor and through Gowerton to the top of the traffic-free trail that drops ever so satisfyingly down through fine broadleaf woodland to the cyclepath along the wide sweep of Swansea Bay. The route into Swansea finishes at the Maritime Quarter and the splendid waterfront. Alternatively, at the point where the route through Clyne Valley Country Park joins the Promenade you may prefer to turn right and head south to the picturesque Victorian seaside resort of Mumbles where there is a wide choice of places to eat or to stay.

Places of interest

LLANELLI MILLENNIUM COASTAL PARK
Few areas in the country have undergone such a stunning transformation. In just a few short years the scars left by the dozens of steel, tinplate and other giant works which dominated the northern shoreline of the Loughor Estuary have been swept away and replaced with the 14-mile Millennium Coastal Park. It is now a mixture of harbours, dune-backed beaches, salt marshes, fenland, tidal basins, woodland and wide open spaces, a model of bio-

The marina at Burry Port

Bike Shops

County Cycles
Swansea Road, Llanelli
01554 775151

Halfords Superstore
Parc Trostre, Llanelli
01554 758538

Wheelies
The Marina, Swansea
01792 464005

Action Bikes
St David's Square, Swansea
01792 464640

Schmoos Cycles
Lower Oxford Street, Swansea
01792 470698

Wheelies Cycles
Uplands Crescent, Swansea
01792 644928 / 472612

Swansea Cycle Centre
Wyndham St, Swansea
01792 410710 / 655440

Cycleworld
Enterprise Park, Swansea
01792 702555

Halfords Superstore
Enterprise Park, Swansea
01792 796601

West Wales Cycles
Morriston Cross, Swansea
01792 534030

diversity, sustainability and habitat conservation.

SANDY WATER PARK

This is where it all began - the former heart of Llanelli's steel trade and the catalyst for the entire coastal regeneration project. The steelworks closed in 1980 with a devastating loss of jobs. The first project of the Welsh Development Agency was to flatten the old steelworks and create Sandy Water Park, based around a 16-acre lake. A Millennium Coastal Park Visitor Centre will soon be built here.

WILDFOWL & WETLANDS CENTRE

The Millennium Wetlands is one of the most important wildlife habitats ever created in Wales. It transformed 250 acres of rough pasture and marsh into a series of lakes, ponds and water features by using fresh recycled water. The wetlands are

The new cycle bridge at Penclacwydd, west of Loughor

Llanelli Millennium Coastal Park

already attracting species lost to the area for 200 years. Other attractions include the Millennium Discovery Centre, a swan maze, water vole city, otter holt, water lily park and a children's activity centre. Three miles of walkways guide you through the saltmarsh and reeds, without disturbing a stunning array of birdlife which includes ducks, geese, flamingo, curlew, lapwing, peregrine falcon, kingfishers, bittern and all five species of British owl. There is free entry for cyclists in the summer holidays.

SWANSEA

Second only in status and size to Cardiff, the 'lovely, ugly town' of Dylan Thomas's boyhood now boasts one of Europe's most stunning and successful waterfront developments. In the 19th century Swansea was caught up in the great period of industrial expansion, serving as a port for the local metal-producing industries. The docklands fell into decline in the 20th century only to be reborn again when the city built the new Maritime Quarter, the centrepiece of which is a 600-berth marina at the old South Dock.

DYLAN THOMAS CENTRE

Dylan Thomas, one of Wales' most famous literary figures, was born in the Uplands area of Swansea. The house at 5, Cwmdonkin Drive, and many other landmarks associated with his early life and writings can now be discovered through publications which follow the Dylan Thomas trails, including the city centre and the Uplands. There is a permanent exhibition 'Man and Myth' at the Dylan Thomas Centre which is situated on the banks of the River Tawe, adjacent to the city's Maritime Quarter.

www.visitwales.com

Llanelli Millennium Coastal Park

Refreshments

KIDWELLY
Lots of choice
Cafe at the Pembrey Country Park Visitor
Centre
Pubs just off the route in Burry Port and
Pwll

LLANELLI
Lots of choice
Cafe at the Wildfowl & Wetlands Centre
Cafe at the marina

GOWERTON
Lots of choice

LOUGHOR
Ship & Castle PH
Railway Inn on the Clyne Valley cyclepath

SWANSEA
Lots of choice

Accommodation

PEMBREY
Four Seasons GH
Gwscwm Road
01554 833367

Ashburnham Hotel
Ashburnham Road
01554 834455

BURRY PORT
Harbour House B&B
The Harbour
01554 833414

LLANELLI
Awel-Y-Mor GH
Queen Victoria Road
01554 755357

Southmead GH
Queen Victoria Road
01554 758588

Llanelli Millennium Coastal Park, with the Gower behind

MUMBLES (SWANSEA)

St Annes Hotel
Western Lane
01792 369147

Waters Edge Hotel
Mumbles Road
01792 401030

Carlton Hotel
Mumbles Road
01792 360450

The Coast House GH
Mumbles Road
01792 368702

Shoreline Hotel
Mumbles Road
01792 366233

SWANSEA

The Grosvenor House GH
Mirador Crescent
01792 461522

Mirador Guest House
Mirador Crescent
01792 466976

Hurst Deane Guest House
Sketty Road
01792 280920

Alexander Private Hotel
Sketty Road
01792 470045

Ael-y-Bryn House GH
Bryn Road
01792 466707

Crescent Guest House
Eaton Crescent
01792 466814

Devon View GH
Oystermouth Road
01792 462008

43

MAJOR CLIMBS

The route is flat from Swansea to Neath and anything but from Neath to Pontypridd!

1 The first major climb, the longest and toughest on the whole Celtic Trail starts at close to sea level on the northern edge of Neath and, with the exception of a couple of short flat or downhill sections, continues over 12 miles to the highpoint of 1970ft (600m).

2 There are two shorter climbs after descending from the highpoint: 230ft (70m) after Lluest wen Reservoir and 295ft (90m) after crossing the A4233 (the Aberdare-Porth road).

TRAFFIC-FREE SECTIONS

Much of this stage is traffic-free. The most attractive sections are the Neath Canal ✳ from Briton Ferry to Tonna (easy!) and the High Level Route ✳✳ through the forestry between Mosshouse Wood (northeast of Neath) and Llanwonno, northwest of Pontypridd (very challenging!). There is a short traffic-free section north of Pontypridd to Cilfynydd.

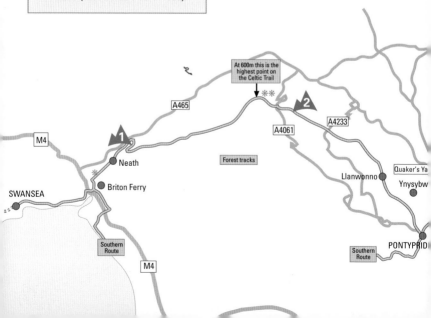

STAGE 5

Swansea to Quaker's Yard (north of Pontypridd) via the High Level Route

44 MILES - STRENUOUS

Swansea Promenade

A greater contrast could hardly exist between the middle section and the two end sections of this stage on the Celtic Trail: the start and finish are dominated by busy roads, bridges, waterways and industrial estates and are largely flat; as a complete mirror image, the middle part includes the longest climb on the whole Celtic Trail, taking you to the highest point of the National Cycle Network in Wales and passes through remote and spectacular woodland with little sign of habitation for mile after mile, until reaching the hamlet of Llanwonno, a few miles from Pontypridd. It must be stressed that the High Level Route is a strenuous challenge on remote forest roads and moorland tracks which should only be undertaken on mountain bikes or hybrids. As it climbs to almost 2000ft you should be prepared for a big drop in temperature at the top. Please go prepared for a change in the weather, ie carry waterproofs and warm clothing and ensure you have the basic tools and a spare inner tube to fix any puncture or breakdown.

Public transport to Swansea

National Rail Enquiries
Telephone: **08457 48 49 50**
Online: **www.nationalrail.co.uk** or
www.walesandborderstrains.co.uk
Normally only two bikes are allowed on a train. You can make a reservation.

Other useful train stations:
Neath, Briton Ferry, Pontypridd.
This is one section where the train really comes into its own if you are just looking for a day ride: there are a variety of train companies providing fast and regular services to Swansea and Neath. By travelling from east to west on the train you are likely to be helped by the prevailing westerly winds on your bike ride back to your starting point. Two of the most attractive (if challenging) options are to catch the train from Cardiff or Newport to Neath and cycle back on the High Level Route to Pontypridd then either the Taff Trail back to Cardiff or the Sirhowy Valley / Monmouthshire & Brecon Canal route (Celtic Trail) back to Newport.

Tourist Information

SWANSEA
01792 468321
tourism@swansea.gov.uk
PONTYPRIDD
01443 409512

www.visitwales.com

The exit from Swansea can hardly be described as pretty but there is no realistic alternative to the narrow coastal strip that carries the A483 and the segregated cycleway that runs parallel to it. Keep the following things in mind: it is only 5 1/2 miles from the centre of Swansea to the start of the peaceful Neath Canal towpath; you are heading east so the wind is likely to be at your back; although noisy, the trail is largely set away from traffic; and for inspiration -

The start of the offroad section of the High Level Route, above Neath

look to the wooded hills that lie ahead! There are long-term plans to use the towpath of the Tennant Canal as an alternative route between Swansea and Neath.

The Neath Canal comes as balm to the soul: the well-made towpath carries you away from the M4 alongside banks covered in wildflowers. It is a fine, stress-free way of travelling into and through Neath. The generally flat nature of the route that has been a dominant feature for the last 35 miles comes to an abrupt finish at the start of Fairylands Road, the minor no-through-lane that rises steeply from the B4434 towards the vast forestry holdings up above the old coal mining valleys. The gradient is at times very steep and if you are not walking you will certainly be using your easiest gear. There are a few vehicles on the tarmac section so avoid riding two abreast on this stretch.

Bike Shops

Halfords Superstore
Cadoxton, Neath
01639 635731

Dare Valley Cycles
Canon Street, Aberdare
01685 886797

Rhondda Cycle Centre
High Street, Treorchy
01443 776584

Bicycle Doctor
Pontypridd Road, Porth
01443 683052

Broadway Cycle Co
Broadway, Pontypridd
01443 402772

Halfords Superstore
Ynysyngharad Road, Pontypridd
01443 485607

The High Level Route

The tarmac (and the worst of the first climb) ends where the pylons and power lines cross the trail. You have now climbed over 800ft (244m) and can look forward to a respite with a relatively flat section through the first part of the woodland. The second steep climb takes you across a moorland stretch with wide views down into the Vale of Neath and the hills rising to the north. This is the most exposed section of the whole ride: there are plans to improve the surface. You soon rejoin the network of wide, stone, forest roads as you re-enter the woodland.

Keep a close eye out for '47' and 'Celtic Trail' signs as you climb, drop, and climb again passing some fine sculptures. There are magnificent views north towards the Black Mountain and Brecon Beacons. The

Celtic Shelter Artworks are at the halfway stage along the route. You can congratulate yourself on reaching almost 2000ft (600m), the highest point on the National Cycle Network in Wales (it is beaten by just 30ft /10m by the C2C Route in England as the highest point on the whole network!). As you descend from the highpoint to the A4061, a short diversion north along the road will take you to a viewpoint where you can look down over Tower Colliery, the last remaining deep pit in South Wales.

It would be wrong to say it is all downhill from here to Pontypridd as there are still a couple of noticeable hills to climb, either side of the A4223. This is one of only two roads that are crossed between the end of the tarmac above Neath and the hamlet of

Llanwonno. There are glimpses down into Maerdy, set right at the top of Rhondda Fach, once the greatest coal-producing area in the world. The Brynffynon pub is the only chance of refreshment between Neath and Pontypridd and comes before a long descent on tarmac down into the busy town of Pontypridd, dropping almost 1000ft (305m). There are plans for an alternative route dropping down from Llanwonno to Ynysybwl to join the Taff Trail near to Cilfynydd (north of Pontypridd).

The ride leaves Pontypridd on a residential road of terraced houses typical of the Welsh valleys and soon joins a traffic-free path alongside the River Taff. In the future the Celtic Trail and the Taff Trail, which share the same course for 5 miles north of Pontypridd, will continue all the way alongside the river up to Abercynon. For the present the route leaves the banks of the river at Cilfynydd and follows the little-used A4054 for a couple of miles. The wooded hillsides steepen and the trail passes beneath two enormous road bridges spanning the Taff. At Quaker's Yard the Taff Trail and the Celtic Trail divide. Our course lies to the northeast whereas the Taff Trail continues north towards Aberfan and Merthyr Tydfil.

Places of interest

NEATH
The town stands at the gateway to the attractive Vale of Neath and has a long rugby tradition: a plaque outside the Castle Hotel commemorates the inaugural meeting of the Welsh Rugby Union in 1881. Neath Rugby Club - the Welsh All Blacks - has played a notable part in the development of the game in Wales.

The High Level Route

Neath Canal

NEATH BOROUGH MUSEUM
Varied exhibits include finds from the local Roman fort, Nidum, and a life-size model of a Roman cavalryman. Located by the churchyard in the centre of town.

GNOLL COUNTRY PARK, NEATH
Large moss house gardens with grottos, streams and follies, cascades down a wooded slope and an ice house. It is signposted as Moss House Country Park / Gnoll Community Park on the Neath - Tonna road (B4434).

ABERDULAIS FALLS
Lovely waterfalls in a small wooded gorge just off the A465 about 2 miles northeast of Neath. There are the remains of the 19th-century tinplate works which were powered by water. The Visitor Centre interprets the history of the site. They are about 1 mile off the route, but can be accessed via the pleasant, traffic-free canal towpath.

RHONDDA
Although the Celtic Trail passes above the Rhondda valleys, you are only a couple of miles from the top of both Rhondda Fawr at Blaenrhondda and Treherbert and Rhondda Fach at Maerdy and Ferndale. The Rhondda valleys were synonymous with coalmining in the boom years of the 19th century. These narrow, steep-sided valleys were known far and wide as the source of the 'black diamond'. Tightly-packed terrace communities grew up alongside scores of mines in the confined valley floor - the only place where it was feasible to build. The mines have now closed and massive land reclamation schemes have wiped away the debris of decades of intensive coalmining.

RHONDDA HERITAGE PARK, TREHAFOD
The park is based around the former Lewis Merthyr and Ty Mawr colliery sites at Trehafod (between Pontypridd and Porth). Mining equipment, including colliery headgear, has been preserved for posterity. A major exhibition, based on the theme of 'Black Gold' uses state-of-the-art audio visual techniques to tell the story of the Rhondda and South Wales valleys' coalmining communities. This is a 3-mile diversion off the route, along a traffic-free path northwest from Pontypridd.

PONTYPRIDD
This busy valleys town recalls its past at the Pontypridd Historical and Cultural Centre. Set in an imaginatively converted chapel next to the famous 18th-century single-arched stone bridge, the centre tells the story of Pontypridd's heyday during the coal era.

Refreshments

SWANSEA
Lots of choice

NEATH
Lots of choice
NB There are no
refreshment stops between
Neath and Pontypridd with
the exception of the
Brynffynon Inn at
Llanwonno

PONTYPRIDD
Lots of choice

ABERCYNON
Navigation House PH

Accommodation

BRITON FERRY (NEATH)
Tree Tops Guest House
Neath Road, Briton Ferry
01639 812419

NEATH
Cwmbach Cottages GH
Cwmbach Road, Cadoxton
01639 639825

The Castle Hotel
The Parade
01639 641119

ABERDARE
**Dare Valley Country
Park**
Aberdare
01685 874672

Swansea Marina

**YNYSYBWL (NR
PONTYPRIDD)**
**Tyn-y-Wern Country
House**
Ynysybwl
01443 790551

**TREHAFOD (NR
PONTYPRIDD)**
Heritage Park Hotel
Trehafod
01443 687057

The Bertie Inn
Phillips Terrace
01443 688204

QUAKER'S YARD
Y Gweirglodd B&B
Tramroadside
01443 412777

TREHARRIS
**Welsh International
Climbing Centre**
Taff Bargoed Country Park
01443 710749

NELSON
Fairmead GH
Gelligaer Road
01443 411174

HENGOED
Highfields B&B
Tir-y-Berth Farm
01443 862287

www.visitwales.com

MAJOR CLIMBS

1. The route is flat from Swansea through Port Talbot as far as Margam Park.

2. There is a 330ft (100m) climb up through Margam Park.

3. From the outskirts of Pyle to the highpoint on the railway path is another 230ft (70m).

4. The railway path climbs 200ft (60m) from Sarn to Blackmill.

5. There are two steep and unpleasant climbs on the busy A4093 through Glyn Ogwr of 310ft (95m) and 280ft (86m).

6. From Tonyrefail to Pontypridd there are three climbs of 165ft (50m), 360ft (110m) and 200ft (60m).

TRAFFIC-FREE SECTIONS

* Aberavon Seafront Promenade.

** Margam Park.

*** From Pyle to Tondu through Parc Slip Nature Reserve.

**** From Brynmenyn to Blackmill along the railway path (this could easily be extended on to Nant y Moel up the Ogmore Valley).

***** There is a short riverside path to the north of Pontypridd.

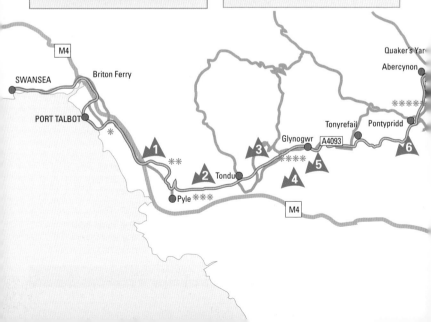

Swansea to Pontypridd via the Southern Route

40 MILES - MODERATE/STRENUOUS

Aberavon Promenade

The Southern Route between Swansea and Pontypridd divides itself into three sections: the first is unavoidably industrial in character, passing right through Port Talbot; the second is largely traffic-free through the delights of Margam Country Park and along specially-built cyclepaths or railway paths to Blackmill; the third and final section uses the network of lanes to climb steeply over the hills that lead to Pontypridd. Be prepared for the hills between Blackmill and Pontypridd: the 1300ft of climbing will come as something of a surprise to anyone expecting this 'low level' route to be easy and flat!

East from Swansea to Margam the course of the Celtic Trail is very much dictated by the topography of the area: there is a narrow, flat coastal strip carrying the motorway and the railway line; set behind this coastal strip are steeply wooded hills rising to over 1000ft. As one might expect, the cycle route choses the flatter course, even if this means sharing the narrow corridor with the noise of the traffic and the industrial landscape of Port Talbot. The route tends to be very well signposted, and with the prevailing wind behind you, this is a section to put your head down and knock off the miles. It will come as a pleasant

Public transport to Swansea

Several train companies operate to Swansea: Virgin, First Great Western and Wales & Borders Trains.
National Rail Enquiries
Telephone: **08457 48 49 50**
Online: **www.nationalrail.co.uk** or
www.walesandborderstrains.co.uk
Normally only two bikes are allowed on a train. You can make a reservation.
Other useful train stations:
Briton Ferry
Baglan
Port Talbot
Pyle
Tondu
Pontypridd, Abercynon, Quaker's Yard (served by Valley Lines)

 Bike Shops

Trailblazer
Station Road, Port Talbot
01639 899699

Cycle Trax
Bridgend Road, Aberkenfig
01656 729211

H R Cycles
Five Bells Road, Bridgend
01656 766006

Broadway Cycles
The Broadway, Pontypridd
01443 402772

Halfords Superstore
Ynysyngharad Road, Pontypridd
01443 485607

surprise to anyone whose experience of Port Talbot is limited to the snapshot of heavy industry seen from the motorway that the seafront overlooking Aberavon Sands is a wonderful, open promenade with wide views out over Swansea Bay.

With its juxtaposition to the heavy industry of Port Talbot, Margam Park is a real highlight. It takes a matter of only two minutes to leave behind the roar of the A48 and the M4 and melt into the delightful broadleaf woodland and lakes of the country park. There is a good chance of refreshment here if you dive off the main route and drop down to the magnificent pile of Margam House. Long term plans will carry the route from Margam Park directly into the back of Pyle to link up with the railway path. In the meantime a short section of the A48 is unavoidable.

The largely traffic-free sections all the way from Pyle to Blackmill are wonderful: the Celtic Trail uses the trackway of the former Dyffryn Llynfi & Porthcawl Railway which was once used to transport coal between Caerau and Porthcawl, then joins a

 Tourist Information

SWANSEA
01792 468321
tourism@swansea.gov.uk

BRIDGEND
01656 654906

PONTYPRIDD
01443 409512

The railway path up Ogmore Vale

specially-built cyclepath that crosses Parc Slip Nature Reserve, using at one point a raised wooden platform to carry the route over a particularly marshy section. At the end of this first long traffic-free section you have the chance to visit Tondu Ironworks Visitor Centre with its adjoining cafe.

It is close to this point that another traffic-free link will take you alongside the Ogmore River into the heart of Bridgend where there are fast rail connections east and west. The route in Tondu that links the end of the traffic-section from Pyle to the start of the next in Brynmenyn is complicated but well-waymarked; keep your eyes peeled for the Celtic Trail and National Cycle Network '4' signs. The railway path northeast of Brynmenyn could be followed all the way up Ogmore Vale to Nant y Moel but our route turns due east at Blackmill.

The next section comes with a warning! Long and patient negotiations are still underway to find an alternative route between Blackmill and the Griffin Inn at Hendreforgan (west of Bryn Golau). In the meantime the route has to use the busy and hilly A4093 for almost 4 miles. It is not pleasant and of all the remaining issues to be resolved along the Celtic Trail this is the top priority. It is hoped that during the next few years the problem will be resolved. To put it into perspective, it is half an hour (or less) on a 220-mile route!

Beyond Bryn Golau and Tonyrefail a series of lanes, at times steep and narrow, seems to cut across the grain of the land, leaving the valley of the River Ely to climb up and over into the Rhondda and Taff Valleys, which link in Pontypridd. If this section comes at the end of your day, be sure to have some reserves left as the hills are unexpectedly tough for a 'low level' route!

Pyle to Tondu traffic-free trail

The ride leaves Pontypridd on a residential road of terraced houses typical of the Welsh valleys and soon joins a traffic-free path alongside the River Taff. In the future the Celtic Trail and the Taff Trail, which share the same course for 5 miles north of Pontypridd, will continue all the way alongside the river up to Abercynon. For the present the route leaves the banks of the river at Cilfynydd and follows the little-used A4054 for a couple of miles. The wooded hillsides steepen and the trail passes beneath two enormous road bridges spanning the Taff. At Quaker's Yard the Taff Trail and the Celtic Trail divide. Our course lies to the northeast whereas the Taff Trail continues north towards Aberfan and Merthyr Tydfil.

Places of interest

MARGAM COUNTRY PARK

The 850-acre country park boasts an Iron Age hill fort, a ruined 12th-century monastery, a restored abbey church with windows by William Morris, a country house with a magnificent orangery and parkland decorated with more than 40 sculptures. Margam Stones Museum has inscribed stones and crosses dating from the 5th to 11th centuries.

PARC SLIP NATURE RESERVE

The Reserve is in a valley bottom area on the watershed between the Ogmore and Afon Kenfig catchment, which has had a history of mining from the 19th century to the present day. Restoration of the land from colliery coal tips and recent opencast coal mining was completed by the late 1980s and is presently managed to enhance natural succession and recreate semi-natural habitats, such as wildflower grassland, ponds, marshes and broadleaved woodland.

TONDU IRONWORKS
It last produced iron in 1895 but now is considered of international importance for industrial archaeology. The primary project aim was to conserve the remaining structure through a programme of engineering and building consolidation measures. Transformations include a heritage centre with visitor facilities, connected by community routes to local centres of population. A new interpretation centre forms an educational and cultural resource and a focus for ongoing community involvement.

Margam House

Refreshments

SWANSEA, BRITON FERRY AND PORT TALBOT
Lots of choice

MARGAM COUNTRY PARK VISITOR CENTRE
tea rooms

KENFIG HILL
Woodstock Inn

BLACKMILL
Fox & Hounds PH

HENDREFORGAN
Griffin Inn

Accommodation

BRITON FERRY (NR NEATH)
Tree Tops GH
Neath Road
01639 812419

ABERAVON
Aberavon Beach Hotel
Port Talbot
01639 884949

MARGAM
Ty'n-y-Caeau GH
Margam
01639 883897

BRIDGEND
The Masons Arms Hotel
Bryncethin
01656 720253

TREHAFOD (NR PONTYPRIDD)
Heritage Park Hotel
Trehafod
01443 687057

THE BERTIE INN
Phillips Terrace
01443 688204

TRAFFIC-FREE SECTIONS

The majority of the route from Trelewis to Newport is traffic-free. The three most popular sections are:

✳ Taff Bargoed Millennium Park southeast to Hengoed Viaduct

✳✳ Sirhowy Valley Country Park from Pontllanfraith to Cross Keys.

✳✳✳ Monmouthshire & Brecon Canal from Cross Keys to Newport (or just as far as the Fourteen Locks Visitor Centre to the west of Newport)

At present there is no long stretch of traffic-free path between Newport and Chepstow. There are long-term plans for a route alongside the M4 to the south of Caldicot to link with Mathern (southwest of Chepstow).

MAJOR CLIMBS

🔺**1** A 170ft (50m) climb from Quaker's Yard up a series of zig zags to The Cascades (Trelewis).

🔺**2** The second climb is right at the end of the ride on the approach to Chepstow from Mounton: 200ft (60m) from crossing the bridge over the stream in Mounton to crossing the A466 on the outskirts of Chepstow.

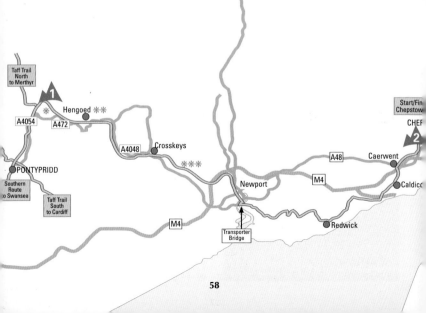

58

Quaker's Yard (north of Pontypridd) to Chepstow via the Sirhowy Valley Country Park

44 MILES - EASY

Dragonfly sculpture at Fourteen Locks Canal Centre

Together with the Llanelli Millennium Coastal Park, the first half of this stage represents one of the greatest success stories of regeneration along the whole of the Celtic Trail. A combination of railway path, canal towpath and newly-built cyclepaths through previously derelict or inhospitable tracts of land has created a magnificent and largely traffic-free route that has enormous appeal to a wide range of people. Once you have climbed up to Trelewis you are faced with a largely downhill, traffic-free ride all the way to Newport. From Newport to Chepstow the way is almost all flat with the exception of a final climb close to the end.

A short steep climb from Quaker's Yard up a series of zig zags takes you past The Cascades, a dramatic water feature

Public transport to Pontypridd / Abercynon

Pontypridd and Abercynon are served by the Valley Lines service between Cardiff and Merthyr Tydfil. There are frequent services.

National Rail Enquiries
Telephone: **08457 48 49 50**
Online: **www.nationalrail.co.uk** or **www.walesandborderstrains.co.uk**
Normally only two bikes are allowed on a train. You can make a reservation.

Other useful train stations:
Ystrad Mynach and Hengoed

Chepstow is on the Newport to Gloucester line. If you wish to travel east from the end of the ride in Chepstow (to Bristol or London) you will need to catch the train to Severn Tunnel Junction and change there. Alternatively you may wish to continue by bike over the old Severn Bridge and follow Route 4 to Bristol, Bath and beyond.

Tourist Information

PONTYPRIDD
01443 409512
NEWPORT
01633 842962
CHEPSTOW
01291 623772

carrying the Bargoed Taff down the valley and beneath a handsome new footbridge over the river. The next section is all newly-built, running parallel with part of the freight railway line which links Ystrad Mynach to Merthyr Tydfil. There are large areas of newly landscaped land, regenerated from old industrial workings. Across the mighty Hengoed Viaduct, spanning the Rhymney River, with its magnificent 'Wheel of Drams' artwork, the Celtic Trail briefly runs parallel with the busy A472 before diving off once again into the secret world of the traffic-free cyclepath, this time following the wooded delights of the Sirhowy Valley. One of the best views along this section of the Celtic Trail can be appreciated from the top end of the Country Park as the lovely wooded valley swings round in an arc to the east.

Shortly after leaving the park and joining the road through Cross Keys you should keep an eye out behind you to your left for a magnifcent mural covering a whole wall. You soon cross a fine park in the centre of town then hop across a series of residential roads and a railway line to join the Monmouthshire & Brecon Canal which is followed all the way to Newport. Some of the canal locks have been restored, although so many sections have been completely built over that it seems unlikely that it will ever be a fully functioning canal again. This is not really a problem for you as a cyclist, as the towpath is generally in very good condition. The canal loses height quickly alongside the Fourteen Locks, briefly runs parallel with the M4 then joins a path alongside the River Usk right into the heart of Newport.

The canal towpath alongside the Fourteen Locks, north of Newport

The final section of the Celtic Trail is bracketed by highlights at either end of the ride with some easy flat cycling in between. The western highlight, at the start of the ride, is the Transporter Bridge, an amazing structure which dominates the Newport skyline. It is a gondola which carries vehicles, cyclists and pedestrians from one side of the Usk River to the other. Please note that there is no service on Sunday mornings. At the western end, Chepstow Castle represents a fine and dramatic finishing point for the ride. You will have plenty of places in Chepstow to choose for your celebrations if you have made it all the way from Fishguard.

East from the Transporter Bridge the route is easy cycling on quiet flat lanes but after the plethora of industrial heritage sites and natural beauty of the last few days, this section is relatively tame with rough pasture, drainage ditches and views of the Llanwern Steel Works! There are opportunities for refreshments in Redwick, Caldicot and Caerwent, near to the old Roman ruins. The ride really takes wings in the very final stages as you climb up from Mounton through beautiful rolling countryside of fields, hedgerows and broadleaf woodland, leaving you with a wonderful and exhilarating swoop down through Chepstow's medieval streets to the dramatically set castle overlooking the River Wye. Congratulations to all of you who have made it end to end from the Pembrokeshire Coast to Chepstow Castle. Come back and ride the other parts of the Celtic Trail that you did not have a chance to see this time round!

www.visitwales.com

Places of interest

LLANCAIACH FAWR LIVING HISTORY MUSEUM

The guides speak in authentic 17th century English and describe events as they see them - story lines run very much like a 'soap opera', reflecting the different events in the servants' lives and the events taking place in the country. Visitors can try the colonel's armour and weaponry, dress up in period costume, visit the panelled Ludwigsburg Rooms or even take a turn in the stocks. Llancaiach Fawr has an annual programme of special events - ranging from archery and falconry to 'An evening with Colonel Prichard' and 'Tales at the Fireside'.

SIRHOWY VALLEY COUNTRY PARK

Beautiful and varied country park, one of the largest in Wales, covering 1000 acres. There are woodland and riverside walks, a picnic area, a Visitor Centre and a memorial chapel to the poet Islwyn.

CROSS KEYS

This village of mainly terraced houses stands at the southern end of the Ebbw valley, once clamorous with industry. With the closure of the coalmines that were at the heart of its economy, the essential beauty of the area has been re-established. The steep-sided hills above, now clothed with conifers, lead to open moorlands.

THE GWENT LEVELS

This area is the most extensive ancient fenland in Wales. Narrow lanes run through this reclaimed land, criss-crossed with ditches and rich in marsh plants and birdlife. The sea was once some distance away and what was once dry land lies beneath the waters of the Severn Estuary.

CALDICOT CASTLE

The castle was founded in the 12th century and was built in stages over the next 200 years. It fell into disuse but was restored by the Victorian barrister Joseph Cobb who carefully researched its original appearance.

CAERWENT

The village was once Venta Silurum, 'the market town of the Silures', the tribe conquered by the Romans around AD 75, after 25 years of hostilities. Long sections of the Roman perimeter walls remain. A plaque in the church lychgate commemorates a remarkable Victorian civil engineer, Thomas Andrew Walker, who built the Manchester Ship Canal and the Severn Railway Tunnel.

CHEPSTOW

The town has retained its medieval street pattern. Town Gate, built in the late 13th century, stands at the top of the High Street. A well-preserved section of the town wall - known as the Portwall - lies nearby. Chepstow stands at the southern end of Offa's Dyke Path, a 168-mile walk along the England / Wales border to Prestatyn in North Wales. The Wye Valley Walk runs for 52 miles from Chepstow to Hereford.

CHEPSTOW CASTLE

There was an Iron Age hillfort in the vicinity and the Romans built a bridge across the River Wye near here, but its real history begins with the Norman Conquest. The high bluff commanding the river was of such strategic importance that in 1067, just one year after the Norman Invasion, work began on the Great Tower, which was the earliest stone castle in Britain. The defences were gradually extended over the succeeding centuries and Chepstow was held for the King at the outbreak of the Civil War.

onmouthshire & Brecon Canal, north of Newport

Refreshments

QUAKER'S YARD
Quaker's Yard Inn,
Taff Trail Inn

HENGOED
Maesycwmmer Inn

**SIRHOWY VALLEY
COUNTRY PARK**
Ynys Hywel Visitor Centre

CROSS KEYS
Lots of choice

NEWPORT
Lots of choice

REDWICK
Rose Inn

CAERWENT
Coach & Horses PH

CHEPSTOW
Lots of choice

Accommodation

QUAKER'S YARD
Y Gweirglodd B&B
Tramroadside
01443 412777

TREHARRIS
**Welsh International
Climbing Centre**
Taff Bargoed Country Park
01443 710749

NELSON
Fairmead GH
Gelligaer Road
01443 411174

HENGOED
Highfields B&B
Tir-y-Berth Farm

01443 862287

NEWPORT
Craignair
Corporation Road
01633 259903

Annesley House
Caerleon Road
01633 212918

Ashburton
Caerleon Road
01633 211140

Knoll GH
Stow Hill
01633 263557

St Etienne GH
Stow Hill
01633 262341

REDWICK
**Brick House Country
GH**
North Row
01633 880230

CALDICOT
The Lychgate B&B
Church Road
01291 422378

CHEPSTOW
Beaufort Hotel
Beaufort Square
01291 622497

Castle View Hotel
Bridge Street
01291 620349

George Hotel
Moor Street
01291 625363

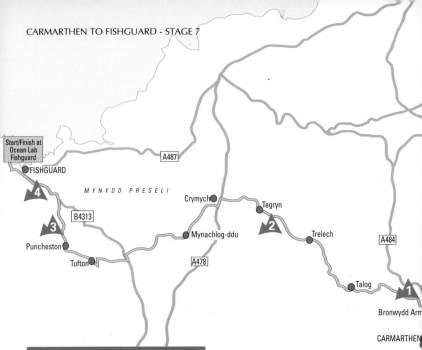

Start/Finish at
Ocean Lab
Fishguard

FISHGUARD

MYNYDD PRESELI

A487

Crymych

Tegryn

B4313

Mynachlog-ddu

Trelech

A484

Puncheston

Tufton

A478

Talog

Bronwydd Arm

CARMARTHEN

MAJOR CLIMBS

1 From Bronwydd Arms (north of Carmarthen) to Bwlchnewydd you are faced with the toughest and longest climb of the day - 530ft (162m) in little over 2 miles.

2 There are many climbs (too many to mention!) ranging from 100ft (30m) to 330ft (100m) between Talog and Puncheston. The worst is over by the time you get to Crymych (just over halfway from Carmarthen to Fishguard).

3 The last main climb of the day (rewarded by fantastic sea views!) rises 485ft (148m) from Puncheston up on to the flanks of Mynydd Cilciffeth.

4 Just when you thought it was all over there is a short steep climb of 125ft (38m) between Llanychaer and Fishguard.

TRAFFIC-FREE SECTIONS

None, although the traffic-free circuit of Llys-y-Fran Reservoir is just off the route, to the south of Tufton.

Carmarthen to Fishguard via the Preseli Hills

44 MILES - STRENUOUS

Alternative 1: Completing the loop from Carmarthen back to Fishguard via the Preseli Hills (to be used in conjunction with Stages 1, 2 & 3)

This part of the Celtic Trail is not for the faint-hearted! It is a tough and beautiful section along remote and quiet lanes passing close to the Preseli Hills with a whole series of climbs to test your fitness. If you are doing the Carmarthen - Fishguard - Pembroke - Carmarthen Loop then you can console yourself that once this day is over, the rest will be relatively easy by comparison!

The ride starts with an easy gradient along the A484 road towards Cardigan: it is at Bronwydd Arms that the real fun begins! This is the longest hill of the day with some very steep sections. You gradually rise up above the valley until you are rewarded with 360-degree views over a landscape of rounded hills, a patchwork of fields bounded by hedgerows with the occasional copse of broadleaf woodland.

Enjoy the brief undulating plateau that takes you past the golf course before entering the rollercoaster section down to Talog and beyond to Trelech, Tegryn and Crymych. This is a land of rich pastures and high hedgerows with solid stone-built

Public transport to Fishguard

Train from Swansea.
National Rail Enquiries
Telephone: **08457 48 49 50**
Online: **www.nationalrail.co.uk** or **www.walesandborderstrains.co.uk**
Normally only two bikes are allowed on a train. You can make a reservation.
Other useful train stations:
Carmarthen

Tourist Information

CARMARTHEN
01267 231557
carmarthentic@carmarthenshire.gov.uk
FISHGUARD
01348 873484

Bike Shops

Hobbs Cycles
Johnstown, Carmarthen
01267 236785
Ar De Feic
Heol Y Brenin, Carmarthen
01267 221182
Halfords Superstore
Parc Pensarn, Carmarthen
01267 237087
Premier Sports (limited repairs)
High Street, Fishguard
01348 873880

farmhouses dotted along the route. Your only chance of refreshments in the 16 miles between Carmarthen and Trelech is at the stores in Talog. After this there are pubs at Trelech (Beca Tavern), Tegryn (Butchers Arms) and Crymych (Crymych Arms Hotel and London House Hotel). It says something for the remoteness of the Carmarthen to Fishguard section that Crymych, with its small handful of shops, is the biggest settlement along the 46 miles.

www.visitwales.com

The stretch that follows Crymych is probably the most scenic of the entire section: an unfenced, undulating road runs between bright yellow gorse bushes and boulders with a dramatic backdrop of the Preseli Hills rising to 1760ft (536m). It was from here that the mighty stones were transported to create Stonehenge, over 240 miles away. There are few opportunities for refreshments between Crymych and Puncheston: the only pub on the route is the Tufton Arms at Tufton with a couple of others just off the route at Rosebush and Maenclochog.

Puncheston is located at the start of the final major climb of the section. Although the sea may have been glimpsed previously, it is at the top of the climb following Puncheston that you are first rewarded with panoramic coastal views: according to which way you turn your head you may be looking out over Fishguard Bay, Cardigan Bay, St George's Channel or the Atlantic Ocean!

The wonderful fast descent takes you down from the slopes of Mynydd Cilciffeth into the wooded Gwaun Valley. Just when you

Places of interest

PRESELI HILLS

The shattered rocks at the peak of Foel Cwmcerwyn rise to 1760ft (536m), with views across the Pembroke peninsula as far as the Devon coast. Massive stones were transported from here for 240 miles to Stonehenge.

GWAUN VALLEY

The scattered inhabitants of this sparsely populated valley come together on 13th January to celebrate the New Year. This custom is explained by their adherence (for the New Year at least) to the old pre-1752 calendar, which ran 12 days behind the times. Today's inhabitants are still happy with the old ways at year's end, celebrating with a feast of goose and plum pudding while the children collect 'calennig', gifts of money and fruit.

FISHGUARD

See page 17

thought all the climbing was over there is one last short and steep hill after crossing Crinei Brook, soon after passing the Bridge End Inn in Llanychaer. After the remoteness of the past 46 miles, Fishguard seems like a positive metropolis with its shops, pubs, cafes, banks and every other service! You have reached the coast and will stay within 7 miles of the sea for the whole trip back to Carmarthen (or on to Swansea).

Refreshments

CARMARTHEN
Lots of choice

TALOG
stores: open Monday to Friday all day and Saturday morning till 1200

TRELECH
Beca Tavern. Stores open Mon–Sat (closed Wed & Sat pm)

TEGRYN
Butchers Arms PH

CRYMYCH
Crymych Arms Hotel, London House Hotel, fish and chips, Chinese takeaway, stores

TUFTON
Tufton Arms PH

PUNCHESTON
Drovers Arms PH, stores

LLANYCHAER
Bridge End Inn

FISHGUARD
Lots of choice

Accommodation

CARMARTHEN
The Drovers Arms Hotel
Lammas Street
01267 237646

Y Dderwen Fach GH
Priory Street
01267 234193

Meiros Hall B&B
Waterloo Terrace
01267 222708

MYNACHLOG-DDU
Dolau Isaf Farm
01994 419327

MAENCLOCHOG
Twmpath Guesthouse
01437 532990
Trepant Farm
01437 532491

PUNCHESTON
Penygraig Farmhouse
01348 881277

TRAFFIC-FREE SECTIONS

* Railway path from near Tumble down to Sandy Water Park in Llanelli.

** Millennium Coastal Park from Llanelli to Loughor Bridge.

*** Railway path from Gowerton through Clyne Valley Country Park.

**** Promenade along the seafront in Swansea.

MAJOR CLIMBS

1 Gently undulating 8-mile section from Carmarthen to Llanarthne then 280ft (85m) climb to National Botanic Garden.

2 Second climb (265ft/81m) from Porthyrhyd to Capel Seion.

3 Third climb (330ft/100m) from crossing the valley formed by the Gwendraeth Fawr up to the railway path (southwest of Tumble).

4 Llanelli to Swansea is almost all flat with one gentle climb after Gowerton before the descent through Clyne Valley Country Park to Swansea Bay.

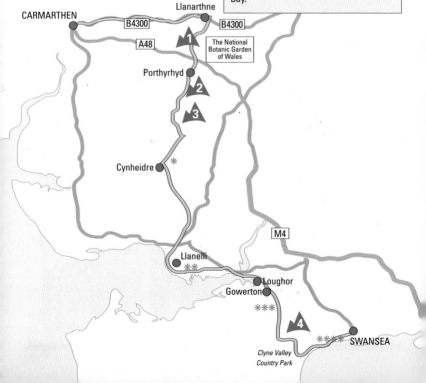

STAGE 8

Carmarthen to Llanelli and Swansea

42 MILES - MODERATE

The National Botanic Garden of Wales

Alternative 2: From Carmarthen via Swiss Valley to Llanelli & Swansea

This is the northern of the two options running from Carmarthen to Llanelli. The two main attractions of this inland route are the National Botanic Garden of Wales at Middleton Hall and the wonderful traffic-free descent down the dismantled railway from near Capel Seion to Sandy Water Park in Llanelli. You may choose to do this section as part of a loop starting and finishing in Carmarthen or Llanelli or

even Swansea (with the section from Swansea to Llanelli repeated on the outward and return parts of the ride). It is described below from west to east but there should be no problem following the route from east to west as it is well signposted in both directions.
Heading east from Carmarthen, the first 8 miles to the minor road turn off after Llanarthne are along a B road that at times

Public transport to Carmarthen

Wales & West trains from Swansea.
National Rail Enquiries
Telephone: **08457 48 49 50**
Online: **www.nationalrail.co.uk** or
www.walesandborderstrains.co.uk
Normally only two bikes are allowed on a
train. You can make a reservation.
Other useful train stations:
Llanelli
Swansea

Tourist Information

CARMARTHEN
01267 231557
carmarthentic@carmarthenshire.gov.uk
LLANELLI
01554 772020
SWANSEA
01792 468321
tourism@swansea.gov.uk

*The new cycle bridge at Penclacwydd,
west of Loughor*

can be busy with traffic. The good news is
that the gradients are fairly gentle and the
wind is likely to be behind you. It is a land
of rich pastures and clumps of broadleaf
woodland. There are a couple of chances of
refreshment at Llanarthne before a climb
of almost 300ft (91m) takes you around
the back of the vast glass dome that is the
centrepiece of the National Botanic
Garden. A newly-built traffic-free path
runs right around the perimeter of the
gardens and links to a segregated
cyclepath alongside the B4310 to
Porthyrhyd, again offering two pubs for
refreshment.

The steepest climbs of the section follow

Porthyrhyd. Tiny lanes with high hedgerows
take you up to Capel Seion, then, after a
fast descent down into the valley formed
by the Gwendraeth Fawr, a second climb
leaves you high up on the traffic-free
railway path that will take you all the way
to Llanelli. This is a cyclepath made in
heaven! A gentle descent of almost 600ft
(183m) over 11 miles leaves you with a big
grin on your face as you come down into
Sandy Water Park.

The route to Swansea goes past the
superbly set Wildfowl & Wetlands Centre
which has started attracting back many
species of bird not seen in these parts for
decades. A safe crossing of the A484 via a

new pedestrian bridge leaves you with a few miles on road, into Loughor and through Gowerton to the top of the traffic-free trail that drops ever so satisfyingly down through fine broadleaf woodland to the cyclepath along the wide sweep of Swansea Bay. The route into Swansea finishes at the Maritime Quarter and the splendid waterfront redevelopment.

Places of interest

Middleton Hall National Botanic Garden

The National Botanic Gardens of Wales, the first to be built in the UK for 200 years, are set in the former Middleton Estate. Its centrepiece is the Great Glasshouse, the largest single-span glasshouse in the world, surrounded by lakes, cascades and woodlands.

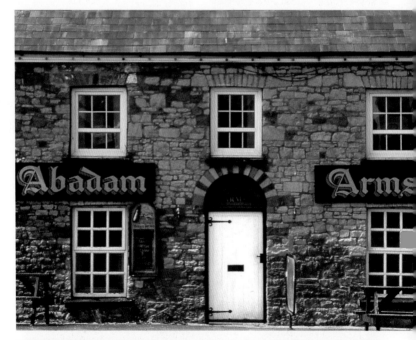

www.visitwales.com

73

Bike Shops

Hobbs Cycles
Johnstown, Carmarthen
01267 236785

Ar De Feic
Heol Y Brenin, Carmarthen
01267 221182

County Cycles
Llandeilo Road, Cross Hands
01269 845656

County Cycles
Swansea Road,
Llanelli 01554 775151

Wheelies
The Marina, Swansea
01792 464005

Action Bikes
St David's Square, Swansea
01792 464640

Schmoos Cycles
Lower Oxford Street, Swansea
01792 470698

Wheelies Cycles
Uplands Crescent, Swansea
01792 644928 / 472612

Swansea Cycle Centre
Wyndham St, Swansea
01792 410710 / 655440

Cycleworld
Enterprise Park, Swansea
01792 702555

West Wales Cycles
Morriston Cross, Swansea
01792 534030

Halfords Superstores
Parc Trostre, Llanelli   01554 758538
Enterprise Park, Swansea 01792 796601
Parc Pensarn, Carmarthen 01267 237087

Refreshments

CARMARTHEN
Lots of choice

LLANARTHNE
Old Emlyn Arms PH, Golden Grove Arms PH

PORTHYRHYD
Prince of Wales PH, Abadam Arms PH

HOREB
Waun Wyllt Inn

LLANELLI
Lots of choice
Cafe at Wildfowl & Wetlands Centre

GOWERTON
Lots of choice
Railway Inn in Clyne Valley Country Park

SWANSEA
Lots of choice

Accommodation

CAPEL DEWI (NR CARMARTHEN)
Capel Dewi Uchaf Country House
01267 290799

NANTGAREDIG (NR CARMARTHEN)
Ty Castell
Station Road
01267 290340
Dolau GH
Felingwm Isaf 01267 290464

HOREB (NR LLANELLI)
Waun Wyllt Inn
Horeb Road 01269 860209

LLANELLI
Awel-Y-Mor GH
Queen Victoria Road 01554 755357
Southmead GH
Queen Victoria Road 01554 758588

Short Breaks along the Celtic Trail

Carmarthen - Fishguard - St David's - Haverfordwest - Pembroke - Tenby - Carmarthen

TOTAL DISTANCE FOR FULL CIRCUIT - 146 MILES

An obvious circuit using the two alternative routes between Fishguard and Carmarthen. The full circuit is on the NCN so it will be waymarked. Doing the ride in an anti-clockwise direction is suggested to minimise the time cycling into a westerly wind: this would be largely restricted to the leg from Carmarthen to Fishguard via Trelech.

Distance
Total for full circuit - 146 miles
46 miles from Carmarthen to Fishguard via Trelech
100 miles from Fishguard to Carmarthen via Pembroke

Other options
1. Train from Carmarthen to Fishguard, cycle back to Carmarthen via Pembroke (100 miles)
2. Train from Carmarthen to Fishguard, cycle back to Carmarthen via Trelech (46 miles)
3. Train from Carmarthen to Fishguard, cycle to Haverfordwest (41 miles) and catch the train back to Carmarthen
4. Train from Carmarthen to Fishguard, cycle to Pembroke (55 miles) and catch the train back to Carmarthen
5. Train from Carmarthen to Fishguard, cycle to Tenby (68 miles) and catch the train back to Carmarthen
6. Train from Carmarthen to Haverfordwest and cycle back (59 miles)
7. Train from Carmarthen to Pembroke and cycle back (45 miles)
8. Train from Carmarthen to Tenby and cycle back (32 miles)

Highlights
The Preseli Hills - the Pembrokeshire coastline - St David's - Brunel Cycle Route - Pembroke Castle - Tenby - Dylan Thomas' Boathouse - Carmarthen's Roman Amphitheatre

Refreshments
See entries under Stages 1, 2, 3. and 7

Swansea - Llanelli - Swiss Valley Route - National Botanic Garden - Llanarthne - Carmarthen - Kidwelly - Llanelli - Swansea

TOTAL DISTANCE FOR FULL CIRCUIT - 84 MILES

A circuit making the most of the two excellent traffic-free routes out of Llanelli. All on the NCN so it is all waymarked. It is best to do the route anti-clockwise so that prevailing westerly coastal winds are used to help you along from Ferryside to Swansea

Distance
50 miles.
Adding a spur to and from Swansea to make it a lollipop-shape ride adds on 34 miles (total 84 miles).

Other options
1. Train from Swansea to Carmarthen, cycle back via Kidwelly and Millennium Coastal Park (42 miles)
2. Train from Swansea to Carmarthen, cycle back via National Botanic Garden and Swiss Valley Trail (42 miles)
3. Train from Swansea to Whitland, follow B4328 and B4314 south and southeast through Red Roses (non-NCN) to join the Celtic Trail. Follow NCN via Laugharne and St Clears back to Carmarthen and Swansea (72 miles)

Highlights
Carmarthen Roman Amphitheatre - Kidwelly Castle - Pembrey Forest & Country Park - Llanelli Millennium Coastal Park - Wildfowl & Wetlands Centre - Clyne Valley Country Park - Swiss Valley Trail - National Botanic Garden of Wales

Refreshments

SWANSEA
Lots of choice
Railway Inn on the Clyne Valley cyclepath

GOWERTON
Lots of choice

LOUGHOR
Ship & Castle PH
Cafe at the Wildfowl & Wetlands Centre

LLANELLI
Lots of choice

HOREB
Waun Wyllt Inn

PORTHYRHYD
Prince of Wales PH, Abadam Arms PH

LLANARTHNE
Old Emlyn Arms PH, Golden Grove Arms PH

CARMARTHEN
Lots of choice

FERRYSIDE
Lion Hotel, Ship PH, Ferry Cabin, stores

KIDWELLY
Lots of choice
Pubs just off the route in Burry Port and Pwll

www.visitwales.com

Cardiff - Pontypridd - Southern Route via Tondu - Neath - return on High Level Route - Pontypridd - Cardiff

TOTAL DISTANCE FOR FULL CIRCUIT - 66 MILES

A way of integrating the High Level Route into a circuit, taking in the growing number of traffic-free sections on the Southern Route (NCN 4) between Pontypridd and Swansea. The most popular option is the one-way trip from west to east, up over the High Level Route from Neath to Pontypridd.

Distance
66 miles. Adding a spur to and from Cardiff (which is perhaps a better base / start point for train travel) thus making it a lollipop-shape ride, adds on 30 miles (total 96 miles).

Other options
1. Train from Cardiff to Neath then cycle back via High Level Route (46 miles)
2. Train from Cardiff to Neath then cycle back via the Southern Route and Tondu (50 miles)

Highlights
Bryngarw Country Park - Parc Slip Nature Reserve - Bedford Park Ironworks - Margam Country Park - High Level Route - (Castell Coch - Cardiff Castle)

Accommodation and refreshments

CARDIFF
Lots of choice

PONTYPRIDD
Lots of choice
Brynffynon Inn, Llanwonno

NEATH
Lots of choice

BRITON FERRY
Lots of choice

PORT TALBOT
Lots of choice

MARGAM COUNTRY PARK VISITOR CENTRE
tea rooms

KENFIG HILL
Woodstock Inn

BLACKMILL
Fox & Hounds PH

HENDREFORGAN
Griffin Inn